GO PLAY

The Ultimate Road Map to
Winning the Game of Life

DERYCK RICHARDSON

Published by Authors Place Press
9885 Wyecliff Drive, Suite 200
Highlands Ranch, CO 80126
AuthorsPlace.com

Manufactured in the United States of America.

ISBN: 978-1-62865-679-4

Contents

1. Go Play 1

2. Attitude 15

3. Practice 29

4. Letting Go of the Past 43

5. Setting Proper Goals 55

6. Halftime 66

7. Embrace the Assist 74

8. The End Game 84

9. About the Author 94

1

GO PLAY

"Sometimes, when I see my granddaughters
make small discoveries of their own,
I wish I were a child."

- Dr. Seuss

● ● ● ● ● ● ● ●

"Go play guys, dinner will be ready shortly" is a phrase I heard all too much growing up. I have such awesome memories of making up games and making friends with kids of all ages, shapes, colors, and cultures, simply due to playing. Many of the people I associate with today are products of meeting at the local park, or at a neighbor's house. "Hi, I'm D.J. (my nickname growing up), want to play?" The response was rarely no, it was most often times, "sure!"

There was no thought involved with the decision to go play or the response when asked to play. We just made it happen, often times with a huge smile on our faces as we figured out how to have fun. The only objective was to pass time in an entertaining fashion. There were no instructions, there was no road map for what to do. Sure, we had lines that we didn't cross; playing did not involve hurting ourselves or others. Playing did not involve malicious activities that would come back to bite us in the rear end. Playing just involved having fun and using our creativity to involve others in that fun.

Throwball was one of my favorite inventions and one of the greatest games of all time because it evolved with us. It started with a cheap plastic ball, the type that you would find in a bin at your local supermarket, and a shed door. The object of the game was to try to throw the ball past the goalie into the shed door. It started with a broken tree branch as a marker, 10 feet away from the door or so, and a one-on-one match. The thrower had 10 chances to make it past the goalie then the roles were reversed. Sometimes there wasn't even a pre-determined amount of rounds, we just continued to rotate until we found ourselves bored and looked for something else to do.

As throwball evolved its intensity heightened. Two-on-two, three-on-three, and so on. The offense always had the advantage as one of the defenders was always responsible for being in the goal. It started with a certain amount of steps that the offensive player could take before being required to pass, similar to ultimate frisbee, and it became so in depth, in our teen years, that we used 5 second timers. The offensive man had to throw the ball before the timer went off or there was a change of possession.

The change of possession was crucial to game play, as we only had one goal. So the closest person to the goal, from the offense, had to jump into the goal as fast as possible, or there would be a wide open shot. Of course there was still that throwline, that by now had become spray paint in the grass. If you crossed that line, there was a penalty and possession change, but if you threw the ball from 20 feet or so, past the bonus line, it was worth two points. Games went to 12, win by two, and often times there were an abundance of kids waiting for their turn. Teams were calling "next," as if it was a basketball court in the summertime. Oh, and that cheap plastic ball had transitioned into a slightly deflated volleyball complete with sharpie designs designating it as the "Official ThrowBall."

We didn't know we had a business plan in the works. We just knew that we had a game that all of the neighborhood kids loved to play. We had unofficial divisions, for instance, the high school kids could not play the middle school kids. Even though we started playing this game while we were in elementary school, we wouldn't let the little kids play while we were out there, however, we would watch after we were tired, and they wanted to play. There were definitely up and coming stars in the "Throwball Championship Series of the World." The little guys had started to perfect moves that we hadn't even thought of. No look shots and behind the back plays. It was inspirational to watch them perform.

Throwball was a game that was created by two people, my cousin James and myself. We created this game at 9 or 10 years old, and can you believe that we played this game as drunk college students? The ball was now any ball that we could palm with ease, and the goal was anything from the front door of our apartment to a space in between two trees. It was a mobile game that could be played anywhere, all we had to do was use our imagination to create a reasonable sized goal. In fact, as we started having kids we would use our kid's toy soccer goals, and the goalie would have to play from their knees.

Throwball was just one game that we created as kids. We made up armies of action figures, played capture the flag, and created forts out of any object we could get our hands on. We played first-bounce-fly runback where we altered the famous childhood game of first-bounce-fly and added the run back component where whoever caught the ball had to run back to the person launching the ball before getting tagged (or tackled as we grew into our teenage years). Boy did this game help us work on our footwork for high school and college sports.

Qball was a great game that could be played inside. Qball is a trademark I believe. Someone had the idea to make a foam square and call it a ball. We purchased this toy at the local toy store and our imaginations went wild. Four players would sit in a square shaped room and each had a basket of some sort. A desk sized trash can was the most common goal and the object was to get the square shaped ball into an opponent's goal. No look shots and fake outs were vital to success. Everyone was seated, which limited mobility, so all you could do was pay attention, stretch out, and use your arms to protect your basket. Bounce shots became effective and off the wall or ceiling shots were important as well as you had to confuse the person who was guarding the basket you were aiming for.

We created all types of games and played any, and everything, to help us enjoy the company of others. If my brother wasn't around, I had to go play by myself. This also wasn't difficult. I picked up a basketball and worked on my dribbling, or colored, or played with Legos. My imagination was so powerful, at that age, that anything was possible. At some point, that changed. At some point, I started to overthink things, and I had to have direction or instructions to figure out what I was supposed to do. At some point, I lost my imagination.

I'd imagine that all of us have experienced this turning point when it comes to our ability to function without instruction. How many times have you been tasked with the objective of figuring something out on your own? How many times have you thrown the directions away when assembling a piece of furniture, only to realize, you didn't need those instructions. You may have had a screw or two (or 8) left over, but the job was completed and the object worked.

Of course the concept of playing changes as we grow older. Going to play as a toddler is vastly different from going to play as a junior or senior in high school. Once we hit high school, things start to change. We are introduced to peer pressure and the idea that our way may not be socially acceptable. What our friends are doing becomes cool. We begin to judge our own actions by the reactions of others within our circle. What if throwball was deemed "stupid" or "amateur," would we have continued to play it to this day? High school educators must do a better job of encouraging self-development and individuality in my opinion. I know it's our responsibility, as parents, to make sure our children are aware of their internal ability to thrive, but as a society, I believe we can all do a better job. It does, in fact, take a village, to raise a child. One of the most important pieces of that village is our school systems.

Since most of you who are reading this book will not have the luxury of being in a school system that is revamped and begins to encourage diversity and individuality, we have to take it upon ourselves to bring that spark back that we once had as a child. We must utilize resources that are available to us now to retrain ourselves and to ensure that we will become what we've always wanted to become.

Another component that we have lost over the years is the ability to tell our friends that we don't want to play with them. Remember when you were mad at Susie or Johnny? You simply grabbed your ball and went home. Now sometimes this action was justified and sometimes it wasn't, but you knew at that age that you did not want to be around that certain situation. As adults, however, we continue to stay in situations that make us unhappy. Relationships, jobs, neighborhoods, and so many predicaments that we put ourselves in can be resolved if we just pick up our toys and leave.

So many of us do not hang out with the same people we did as a children. I know life takes us in different paths. After high school there seems to be some sort of "big bang" and people just end up in different places. Some of us go to college, some start working right away, some go to the military, some start families fairly immediately, but we should try to connect with those who brought us happiness as a child. Technology makes it easy to follow their lives on social media, but pick up the phone and engage in a conversation. People love to actually talk about their lives and what's going on. We are so caught up in short texts and 140 character tweets that we are leaving out the emotion. We are training ourselves to have short attention spans by only sending and receiving short bursts of information. Grab some popcorn and listen to your friends. Find out how you can help. Tell them about what's going on in your life; it will make you feel good inside.

High school made us think that cliques where how we should associate with other people. For the most part we stayed in these small groups of people and didn't expand our horizons because that's what we felt comfortable with. To some degree it's good that we became diverse with our relationships after our school years because we needed to understand that there is more to life than being associated as a jock or a bookworm. But remember that most of those people in that clique expanded their horizons as well.

I still have the same best friend that I've had since middle school. Greg was my best man in my wedding, and when I need advice, I call on him. He does the same with me; I don't know how many times I've traveled to other states just to help him move. We remain best friends, even though our lives are completely different, and we ended up several thousand miles away from each other. Sure, I spend more time with my local compadres, but when push comes to shove, Greg is who I refer to when I need support. We grew up together and experienced the same things. Go out and find your best friend. The one who you found yourself in trouble with, and laughed with, and cried with, and maybe just don't talk to because life created a barrier. You have the power to take the initiative to break that barrier. I bet that you will be pleasantly surprised by the outcome of catching up with old friends who remind you of the innocent years of childhood.

The sole purpose of this book is to provide you with tools to regain the power to make things work your way. Somewhere along the line we became followers. We suppressed our imagination and buried our creativity. How many great ideas have you had that never got off the ground? I mean the whole spectrum. From, "this is a good little idea," to, "this is an absolute freakin' winner!" What are you waiting for? What is stopping you from being great? Is it really the powers of the world that are holding you back, or is it the reflection that you see every day in the mirror? Why do some people succeed and others fail? Why are you not amongst the ranks of the elite?

Throwball was so influential that as I became an adult I wanted to put together a business plan and market this sport to the masses. There was only one problem. Throwball was essentially an adaptation of the famous Olympic sport, Handball. I had heard of handball before, but the sport was something I pictured with a tennis ball and a wall. Some of us call that Wallball. In 2000 I was flipping through the channels during the Summer Olympics in Sydney and noticed a game that resembled Throwball. "They stole my idea!" I yelled as I quickly called one of my buddies. I was devastated to find out that Throwball wasn't new. The game that was such a good idea, had already been invented. In fact, it had been invented hundreds of years ago and first popped up in the Olympics in 1936. As an innocent child, I didn't know this, I just took a concept that seemed fun and turned it into a sport that all of the neighborhood kids loved to play.

As a child our brains are fresh and uncompromised. We have the ability to dream and become anything we want. We have aspirations of greatness and strive to be doctors, lawyers, athletes, and scientists. Somewhere along the line we have convinced ourselves that this can no longer be done. Somewhere along the line we saw a barrier that seemed impossible to penetrate. Is it really impossible? Do you still not have the ability to become who you always wanted to become? We have one shot at this game called life. So what your first quarter didn't go as planned. So what you are down 20 at halftime. Are you going to play the rest of the game as a defeated participant? Or are you going to wake up and decide to live out your dreams? The worst thing to do is to die with regret. You must live as if you are fighting to become something great, something that you've always wanted to become. You must speak, dress, and walk like the person you want to become. Make the decisions now that your future self will thank you for! Act! Go Play!

ATTITUDE

"I've heard there are troubles of more than one kind; some come from ahead, and some come from behind. But I've brought a big bat. I'm all ready, you see; now my troubles are going to have troubles with me!"

Dr. Seuss

* * * * * * * *

I've heard before that, "the only people without problems are dead people, and then again, they might have the biggest problem of us all!" How true this statement is. Everyone in the world has problems. Problems are colorblind, and they don't care how much money you have or where your family lives. Problems come up every day and we must find the proper way to attack these problems and come out on the winning end.

It all starts with your attitude and mindset. We all know that conditioning is real. Pavlov proved this with his experiment with the salivating dogs. If you've never heard of this experiment, google it. It will blow your mind. A better experiment to outline in this book however is the experiment with the monkeys, the ladder, and the sprinkler. I've heard this story many times, both in college and in the workforce, and I find it amazing how our brains are wired to think to do things, simply because it's been done that way before. Grace Murray Hopper states that, "the most dangerous phrase in the human language is, we've always done it this way."

There was a scientist who put five monkeys in a room. On top of a tall ladder were a few bananas that were obviously tempting to the monkeys. One monkey became very ambitious and began to climb the ladder towards the bananas. As soon as this happened the scientist turned on the sprinklers in the room, and all of the monkeys became cold and wet. Soon, however, the bananas started to look good again, and another monkey decided to climb the ladder. Again, the scientist turned on the sprinklers so that all of the monkeys became soaked with cold water. As the third monkey attempted to climb the ladder, the other monkeys had had enough. They recognized that climbing the ladder, for some reason, triggered the sprinklers. The four remaining monkeys quickly pulled the monkey off of the ladder and began to punch him and scream.

The scientist then replaced one monkey with a new monkey that had not witnessed any of the prior events. The first thing that this monkey notices is the banana at the top of the ladder. As he begins to climb the ladder, the four other monkeys in the room quickly pulled him down and began punching him and screaming. The scientist duplicated this process by adding a second new monkey and taking away one of the original monkeys. The same thing happens as this new monkey is beaten up by all of the monkeys in the cage, including the replacement monkey who has no idea why he was being punched for climbing the ladder.

Eventually, the scientist replaces all of the monkeys and there are five new monkeys. None of these monkeys have experienced the sprinklers as a result of climbing the ladder; however, they all beat any monkey that tries to get to the banana. They had been conditioned to do this simply because the society that they had been introduced to had always operated in this manner. How often are we limiting ourselves from developing further in life simply because society tells us it is not OK?

Many of my friends and colleagues have flirted with network marketing or direct sales. I find it so amusing that we, as people, will go out and buy a product that is endorsed by a celebrity that we have never met, yet we rarely support our friends or family who are trying to start a new business. How many of us have had our ideas shot down by friends and family which leads to our confidence taking such a hit that we just give up? Our friends and family want us to stay where we are on the socioeconomic ladder simply because that's how things have always been. People have always failed in their circle, or never tried and remained stagnant, so it is hard for them to imagine anything different from you. It's not their fault that they doubt you, it's just how they've been conditioned. Even if that is not the case, maybe they have a subconscious belief that we will fail so they don't support us. Which leads to the failure they assume will happen.

Either way, understanding that you are your own biggest fan, is the first step in reprogramming your attitude. You don't rely on them, for the most part, to make everyday decisions anymore. You are no longer a high school student who has to wear Nikes instead of Pumas to fit in. You are an adult, and you are your own person. These people who doubt you will have no skin in the game when it comes to your ambitions. They are not vested in your journey, so they have at most very little knowledge of the game plan that you have come up with. And believe me, you must come up with a game plan for whatever goal you want to accomplish. We will talk about this in later chapters.

The next step to reprogramming your attitude is to dive deep into the science that is the mind. The mind is made up of two major parts: the conscious and the subconscious. The conscious mind is what you are aware of. The thinking mind. This portion of the mind is controlled by you. You have the ability to raise your right hand high in the air. You have the ability to do a jumping jack, simply because you tell your mind to make the body do it. The subconscious mind controls things that you don't have to tell your mind to do. Breath, put your right foot in front of the left foot when walking. This part of the mind controls things that need no instruction or direction.

The beauty of the mind is that the conscious mind has the ability to control and retrain the subconscious mind. If your friends and family are repeatedly telling you that you can't succeed, your subconscious mind will start to believe it. You become lazy when attempting to accomplish your goals. You start out working diligently on a project, but as the weeks go on, you feel discouraged, often times giving up. Your subconscious mind has now gone into autopilot, filling your mind with doubt. One of the easiest ways to reprogram yourself is to speak to yourself. Auditory senses are extremely powerful, and we must utilize them when training our mind to convert from a negative thinker to a positive thinker. This is the reason why so many motivational speakers utilize crowd participation. The "repeat after me," and "everyone scream" techniques are powerful because you are tapping into the subconscious mind and reminding it that you are in control.

I recommend starting every day by verbalizing your goals and your dreams. I recommend reminding yourself verbally that you can do this and that you were meant to be great. If you don't believe in yourself, nobody will; I promise you that!

Go back to the days of your childhood for a second. The little things brought you joy. The sound of the ice cream truck in the summertime, the new toy that your parents brought home that came as a surprise, staying up late on the weekends, laughing and joking with a group of friends about meaningless activities, a hug from a parent or a loved one. It didn't take much for us to maintain a positive attitude as a child; we could do anything we wanted, and our brain didn't comprehend that there could be adverse consequences. We just acted. Some of those actions did result in trouble, but I'd bet the overwhelming majority of those actions make up a big piece of our happy memories from childhood.

What brings you joy now? I'm not talking about the type of joy that leaves you hung over the next morning. We can all treat ourselves to an adult beverage every now and again, but what actually brings you joy? Is it time spent with loved ones? Hiking? Enjoying a sporting event? Make sure you reward yourself with things that bring you joy. Being happy is a big part of maintaining a positive attitude. The world is tough, in fact, it is the world that probably helped to destroy your confidence.

The news is filled with depressing story after depressing story. The watercooler talks at work are all negative. Parents at your child's sporting events are complaining about each and every aspect of the game or league. People are flat out negative and it's up to you to stop the negative thoughts now. Remember, if your subconscious mind continues to hear negative things, it will pound those thoughts into your head. You are constantly fighting a battle that you may not even know you are fighting with yourself. In literature and pop-culture we see the image of the angel on one shoulder and the devil on the other. This is an apt depiction of the way you have to train your subconscious. Since you are hearing a plethora of negative content every day, you must begin to think positive thoughts and have positive conversations every day. Fight fire with fire.

So often we get caught up with drama. It's fun, it's sexy, it's interesting. There are more reality shows, showcasing the lives of people who don't get along with each other, than ever before. Ratings on these shows are through the roof. Conspiracy theorists will tell you that "they" want you to get caught up in this culture of drama. They want to suppress your mind with the negatives of the world to keep you from growing as an individual. I say that even if that is the case, you have the power to control your own thoughts. You have the power to turn off the TV and pick up a book. You have the power to watch shows that focus on positive themes rather than negative. This world is scary and dangerous, but it's also beautiful and fulfilling. Whichever world you focus on will be the world you live in.

Another way to reprogram your thoughts is to devote yourself to spreading positivity around you. A smile will go a very long way. In fact, there are studies that show just smiling or laughing will have an impact on your body's chemical reactions. It simply makes you feel good to smile and to laugh. Take control and reap the rewards of having a positive attitude. Watch how you physically feel better and your body has less stress attached to daily activities. Negative things are going to happen, but take the half full approach and only focus on the positive side of any situation. Captain Jack Sparrow says, "it's not the problem that's the problem, it's how you react to the problem, that is the problem."

A popular sales story that sales managers and trainers use is the story of the shoe salesmen in a remote desert country. A shoe company sends two salesmen to the same country where the occupants don't wear shoes. The first salesman comes back to the corporate office to report that he hadn't sold a single shoe. He complains that he should have never been sent to a country where people don't wear shoes. How can he possibly be successful in this environment?

The second salesman comes back and reports that he had broken sales record after sales record. He asked why they had never sent him to a country where people do not wear shoes before. This was the greatest marketing strategy that he had ever heard of. Nobody wears shoes, how could he possibly fail in this environment?

When you are faced with a problem are you looking at the positives? When you have to face adversity, do you automatically look at the worst possible outcome? If so, it's not your fault. You have been programed to think negatively about everything. You have been programed to think that there is no positive solution. But you have the ability to reprogram your mind. You have the ability to train your mind to only see positives. It may feel strange at first. You may feel as if you are not yourself. In fact, you aren't! Your old self was used to complaining, whether internally or verbally. Your old self was used to seeing the glass half empty. Make the decision today to become a new person. Make the decision to embrace your newfound feelings of discomfort. Once your mind gets used to thinking about everything with a positive spin, the benefits will be plentiful.

Less stress leads to more money and more positive relationships. Both positivity and negativity are contagious. Become the leader that spreads positive content. Become the leader that tells people in your circle that you no longer want to listen to the negative vibes. It's up to you to feed your brain and your mind with the seeds that will grow into beautiful flowers. If you only plant seeds of negativity, that is all that will grow. Be aware of the music you listen to. Violence and sin sells because people are drawn to the negative vibes. Reverse that magnetic pull within you and those you love. Make it cool to be positive. Go back to using peer pressure like tactics to be vocal about the power of positive thinking and positive reinforcement.

Finally, think about what you are about to say before you say it. If you were talking to a child, whose mind was still pure and able to be molded into a place of positive vibes, would you say what you are about to say? Pretend that everyone you speak to is in a transitional phase just like you. Act as if your co-workers, family, and friends are transitioning from negative magnets to positive thinkers. Is what you're about to say going to help that journey or harm it? Not only do we need to speak to ourselves in a positive manner, but we also need to speak to others in a positive manner as well. Remember the basic manners that you were taught as a child. Say please and thank you, hold a door open, speak when spoken to, and if you don't have something nice to say, don't say anything at all. These procedures will help you to become a leader within your circle and may influence others to begin to shift their thinking too. Can you imagine what the world would be like if everyone spread positive vibes? It may never happen, but it's possible that within your world and your circle you may live that way. How lucky you will be when that day comes!

PRACTICE 3

"*The more that you read, the more things you will know. The more that you learn, the more places you'll go.*"

Dr. Seuss

* * * * * * * *

Changing your attitude and growing, within yourself, takes practice. It's known that to excel at anything you must practice. The best athletes in the world still rely on their coaches to teach them new things and to keep them working hard. There are several people out there who are good life or career coaches, but I urge you to begin to coach yourself. How often are you talking yourself through situations with confidence? This is crucial to being bought in to your newfound attitude.

Let's look at two examples. Michael Jordan vs. Alan Iverson. We will start with Iverson as most everyone has heard his practice rant. If you haven't, again I refer you to Google or YouTube to take a look at the video. Iverson, a star for the Philadelphia 76ers, had just lost a playoff series that sent him home for the summer. He and coach Larry Brown had a shouting match because Iverson was late for a meeting. Everything calmed down and Iverson agreed to a press conference to assure the media that everything was OK. Except something happened that would make this press conference famous for a lifetime.

Iverson found himself on the defensive end of multiple journalists asking him about his dedication to the team and his effort in practice. Iverson went on a rant where he said the word practice 20 times in the next minute or so. "Practice? We in here talking about practice? I'm supposed to be the franchise player, and we are talking about practice? Practice? Not that game, practice?" The rant goes on, and although we know Iverson was joking and having fun with the media, it reminds us that yes, we are talking about practice.

To be fair, I don't think anyone really doubts the fact that Iverson practiced hard. As a kid with a less than stellar upbringing, he had one focus - basketball. To make it at the professional level and have a career like Iverson, you have to practice day in and day out. I was never in a 76ers practice to watch his effort, but I would imagine it was at a high level most of the time. The question is, is most of the time good enough?

Practice leads to improvement. You have to practice as if you are in the game. Since the game we are talking about is the game of life, a game where there are no do-overs or time-outs, we must practice to improve every aspect of our life: health and nutrition, career growth, relationship building, the list goes on and on. There are several ways to practice in life, but whatever we do, we have to continue to work on our personal development. We are talking about practice, and we are talking about not taking days off when it comes to practice.

What is the best way to practice? I recommend taking at least five minutes per day to read something. Everyone is busy, but I know for a fact that everyone has five minutes every day available to read a chapter of a book or an article on personal development. Even if motivation and personal development aren't your thing, study your craft. If you are a computer programmer, study the latest trends in the coding world. If you are in sales, study the latest trends in the world of sales. This world is constantly changing, and old tactics in your career are evolving on a consistent basis as well.

Let's just take sales for instance, since I am a sales manager and coach by trade. If we think that the tactics and procedures from the 80's are still effective today, then we are very mistaken. Technology tells us the world is different. Email marketing and text message marketing have become more prevalent. Maybe it's not fair to compare today to the 80's, so let's shift our focus to just ten years ago.

Look at a film from ten years ago and notice how it instantly has a feel of being outdated. This same concept can be applied to the tactics that you are using to prospect and sell. Yet we still are using the cold call techniques that we were taught many years ago. We have not realized that the consumer has heard it all before. We have to be constantly changing in our approach or else our sales will become stagnant. There is nothing worse than a stagnant sales professional. Look up books from today, not books that were used while Leno and Letterman still ruled the night air. And if you are reading tactics from the Johnny Carson days, I feel really bad for you. This topic reminds me of one of my favorite sales stories. The story goes as follows:

There once was a lumberjack who was always the best at his trade. As most lumberjacks of his day were bringing down 8-10 trees per day, he was bringing down 15-20. The lumberjack retired and decided that he was going to live happily ever after with his wife. Boy was he in for a surprise when he lost his spark weeks into retirement.

The lumberjack decided that he was not built for retirement. He still had strength and could compete with the best lumberjacks in the country. He soon told his wife that he would be going back to work because he needed to regain a level of self-worth. He just wasn't cut out for baking and reading in his recliner. He was feeling like less of a man.

The lumberjack went and applied at a timber mill and the manager immediately recognized him and knew who he was. He was hesitant to hire the old lumberjack because he knew he was well past his prime. The lumberjack promised that he still had some work left in his body and could compete with the top producer within the timber mill. The manager explained that the top producer was bringing down 12 trees per day. The lumberjack promised that he would beat him if the manager just gave him a chance. The manager had no choice but to see what the old man could still do.

The first week on the job the lumberjack brought down 15 trees every day. The younger workers were in awe, and even the top producer gave the old man praise and showed him the respect that he deserved. The following week the lumberjack brought down an average of 14 trees per day, still well above the next worker in terms of weekly production. The following week his numbers dwindled down to an average of 13 trees per day, then 12 the next week, and 11 the week after. Finally the lumberjack was no longer in first place at the end of the week, and he was extremely frustrated with himself and began to work harder and harder.

The lumberjack went to the manager and assured him that he was not too old and that he was still motivated and driven. He promised to get better and get his average back up as he knew the manager was looking for a super star, not an average employee. The manager looked at the man with a stern voice and said, "I know you have been working hard. I watch you every day, and I see the dedication and focus you have to be a top producer. But let me ask you a question, when was the last time you sharpened your ax?"

The lumberjack looked at him and said, "I haven't. I've been too busy trying to cut down trees."

The morale of the story is that it doesn't matter how hard we work at whatever our objective is, if we are not sharpening our axes, then we are putting ourselves in a position to stay stagnant or move backwards. What are you doing to sharpen your ax? What development tools have you utilized recently? I would urge you to take a look at your skills and abilities and start with focusing on areas that need improvement. Even simple things like vocabulary can make a huge difference when it comes to employability and advancement opportunities within your industry.

Simple tools are available to all of us. Just studying a thesaurus can help expand your vocabulary. It doesn't take long, again, five minutes a day can be powerful. For the sake of marketability this book is written at a high school level, but I assure you I've spent several nights studying words and word play. I never want to be left in the dark when involved in an important conversation. It may sound de minimis, but the prodigious accomplishment of erudition is one of the most inimitable feelings in the world.

Back to our comparable analogy of Jordan vs. Iverson, we have to now look at the positives associated with dedicating your life to practicing at 100%, 100% of the time. Jordan is regarded by most as the greatest basketball player to ever play the game. Many of us know that he was cut from his middle school basketball team. You are probably thinking, "what was wrong with that coach?" The coach, however, has said in several instances that Jordan just wasn't good enough at that time to make his team. Now Jordan could have blamed his coach or blamed others, but he took it upon himself to study the game and practice daily.

The rest is history; we all know how Jordan's legacy played out. However, just because he reached the upper echelon of basketball players doesn't mean he stopped practicing. I would actually bet that the practices became harder as he aged because he had to reinvent himself. By the end of his career, Jordan didn't have the legs that once allowed him to soar over opponents with ease. Jordan had to figure out how to still be as dominating with a newly found jump shot. In the same way, some of our situations change, and we must reinvent ourselves. If we start to reinvent ourselves after we decline in our respective situation then it is too late. Others will have the chance to pass us and leave us in the dust. You have to start reinventing yourself before your decline, so the transition is seamless. You have to practice and invest in yourself. Make a commitment to start doing that now. Make a commitment to start taking yourself to workshops and seminars. Invest in classes and books.

Learn from some of the people who have been in your shoes and are now where you want to be. Mimic success.

Yes, copycat! Let me say that again, mimic success! Kobe Bryant grew up idolizing Jordan. He stuck his tongue out like Jordan; he learned to shoot a fadeaway jumper like Jordan; when his legs were no longer his best asset, he learned to improvise like Jordan, and there are actually some fairly entertaining videos on YouTube that show Bryant making plays in the same exact fashion as Jordan. Jordan's infamous shrug has even been copied by Bryant. He did it the easy way. He saw someone who was where he wanted to be and copied him. His career didn't end up too shabby as a result.

If you see someone in a position that you want to be in, begin to act like they do. Don't be afraid to ask for advice from that person, and don't be afraid to copy what they do. They have to have some information that you don't if they are in a position that you have yet to get to. Most people will see it as flattering. People enjoy mentoring those who appreciate their accomplishments. If that person has some sort of issue with helping you out, ask someone else. Study what they do; practice what they do, and perfect their actions.

There are countless self-development books available online and in bookstores. There are also several online articles that are at our disposal every day. I am not ignorant to the fact that most, if not all, of the topics discussed in this book are not new theories. I don't have the credentials of Tony Robbins or Zig Ziglar, so I understand that there are other options available for you to read. I would like to take this time to say thank you for reading this book. The theme of practice holds true while reading this book though, and you will surely get something out of it. I'm practicing my writing skills on a daily basis and hopefully that practice will make my next book even better.

I urge you to find practice fun and enlightening. I urge you to make it an everyday practice (pun intended). I urge you to habitually practice to continue to improve yourself. There are only so many days that you have left here. You must ask yourself if you want to leave anything on the field. One of the most devastating feelings is knowing that you could have tried harder when it comes to accomplishing a goal. If you've ever played sports then you know that there is no feeling in the world like knowing your team didn't play its hardest and lost. Sometimes it's an accomplishment knowing you tried your hardest and still lost. Any way you look at it, you must try your hardest to get ultimate satisfaction. Self-satisfaction is so important as you start, or continue, your journey of personal growth.

As we wrap up this chapter I'd like to also encourage you to take risks. If an opportunity comes up that you want, accept it. Even if you have no idea how you are going to complete it. Say yes then figure out how to attack the task as you go. Learn on the fly. That's all life is about. Practicing and learning on the fly. Again, there are no time-outs in life. You don't have the luxury of saying, "I would like to accept this opportunity, but please give me two months to train myself so that I can be successful." Say yes, then practice and study how to be successful at whatever project you need to tackle. Living life this way opens up doors that had seemed to be deadbolted prior. Living life this way allows you to become somebody who you dreamed about but didn't realize you were going to become. Get in the car, put on your GPS, and figure out how to get there while you are on the road. Success is a journey, not a destination. Often times the doing is more fulfilling than the outcome! Just make it happen and figure it out on the way. If an opportunity asks you if you want to "play," say, "SURE!"

LETTING GO OF THE PAST

"How did it get so late so soon? It's night before it's afternoon. December is here before it's June. My goodness how the time has flewn. How did it get so late so soon?"

Dr. Seuss

*   *   *   *   *   *   *   *

Life is short; there isn't time to dwell on the past. That game is over; this game has started. Think about how many times we say, "Boy! Time Flies." Time moves so fast that we have to take every opportunity to improve rather than think about what happened in the past, even the good memories. We all know that there are people who have had terrible pasts who have turned out great. We also know that there are people who have had great pasts who turned out not so great. The past is just that, the past.

I've always said, "it's never too late to become who you always wanted to be." I mean that. There are a few crucial steps in making that happen though:

1) Once you say yes to an opportunity, or talk yourself into your own opportunity, come up with a game plan. By no means should you say no because you don't have one yet. You can't just wing it. This life is too important to just wing it. Any business takes a solid business plan to get

off the ground. Any building takes an architect with a wonderful, thought out blueprint before the ground is broken. You have to come up with a game plan, a business plan, or at least start with benchmarks to achieve on the way to conquering your goals. Write them down. Every day make sure you write something down. Type it, text it, email it to yourself, use post it notes, I don't care how you write it down; just do it. You have to be prepared to be great. You have to know what you want to do to be great. Visualize your goals and achieve small victories on the way to becoming great.

2) Start acting like the person you want to become. Dress like that person; talk like that person; walk like that person. Most importantly, make the decisions that person would make. Again, you have to practice. Before a football team is ready to become a Super Bowl champion, they must win the playoffs. Before they win the playoffs, they must win the regular season. Before they take the first snap of the regular season, they

have months and months of practice. Practice becoming the person that you eventually want to become. Or else, you may still become that person, but you won't be very good. Even if the best pre-season football team just skipped practice, skipped the regular season, skipped the playoffs and landed in the Super Bowl, do you think they would be prepared? Of course not. Make sure you begin to train your mind to become the person you want to be.

3) Remember that, "Today was once a year from now and soon will be a year ago." Let that sink in for a minute. Re-read that quote. Actually, I'll help you out. **Today!** As in, look at the calendar and notice what day it is that you are currently reading this line. **Was once a year from now!** Exactly one year ago, today would have been one year in the future. Of course you know that, but what if you had started acting like the person you want to become a year ago. You would have had a one year head start. A year seems like such a long time when we have

to tackle that year, but once we look back to this day last year, it really wasn't that long ago. So again, **Today!** Yes, the same day that you are reading this. **Will soon be a year ago!** It's not too late. Start today so that next year we haven't wasted an entire year coming up with excuses for why we haven't started yet. Or excuses for why we can't do it. Just start today and give yourself a year head start. Look at this date next year, will you see progress or not? Only you can answer that question.

4) Finally, remember the aspect of time. You have to make time for yourself and for your future. You can't just say you are going to do the above mentioned steps. When are you going to do them? Make time every day to invest in your future. You are already doing things throughout the day that are beneficial to someone. When are you making time to do things for yourself? When is it your turn? We can't wait forever to be great, or else we will be old and gray and wondering what happened. Where did the time

go? How many years were wasted not doing the things you wanted to do? How many years were wasted not being the person you wanted to become?

The past is over. Yes, learn from your mistakes. Yes, analyze what you've done, both the good and the bad. Yes, the past is relevant, but it's over. You must use the time we have left in this life to achieve great things. We don't have time to mess around with what could have been. We only have time to realize what we can do with the time left. We are going to die at some point. Will you have left it all on the field or will you have left the field knowing you had more to give? You have to move forward. Life is like riding a bike. As long as you are moving forward, you will stay balanced. As soon as you stop, you fall. Don't fall. Make the best of the talents you have.

Many of you know that I own two businesses. A leads business and an insurance agency. My partner in the insurance business asked me for two straight years to come join him on this journey. The concept sounded nice. Residuals. I was making good money in lead generation, but there was no long term sustainability. There was no passive, residual income. I hesitated for two years before I went in with him. Now that we are thriving in this business, I often wonder why I didn't jump sooner. The answer seems obvious. I was comfortable. I had a business that was doing well; my family was happy, and I had time to golf. I also knew that I wasn't building a future income base though. Yes, it was going to take more time out of my day. More of those 86,400 seconds, but I knew I had to make a little sacrifice to make sure that my family was going to be OK in the future. I had to look ahead to find out where I wanted us to be as my children entered adulthood. I had to start taking my own advice.

There is this stigma that says we have to continue to be the same person that we have always been. We are scared of change. Unfortunately, we have to change. Think about your routines. By routine, I mean what you do on a daily basis. Those routines change anyway. Nowadays I would imagine your routine involves your smartphone (we can leave the debate on this for another book). Ten years ago it probably didn't. Nowadays your TV has DVR, fifteen years ago it didn't. Desktop computers evolved into laptops, which evolved into tablets. Fax machines and house phones are becoming extinct. The point is, we have to evolve with the times as well. So if we have to evolve, why not evolve for the better? Why not pick up some self-help books, or download them to our mobile devices? Why not learn to move forward and leave the past in the dust? Let's make the old, non-motivated person you may think you are extinct.

One of the reasons I started going by Deryck, instead of DJ once I hit 21 or 22 years old, is because I wanted to start fresh. DJ was a 1.85 student. Not because I wasn't intelligent, but because I was too distracted, or lazy (or both) to do homework. DJ barely graduated high school because he was worried about sports and girls. DJ was a teenage father, having his first child at 19 years old. DJ was broke. DJ had evictions and repos and terrible credit by the time he could drink a beer legally. DJ needed to be retired. Deryck on the other hand put himself through college and graduated with a 3.75 GPA. Deryck owns several businesses. Deryck has a beautiful wife and four children in an upscale suburb of Columbus, Ohio. Deryck took two businesses to the INC500 list of fast growing businesses in the nation. Deryck took two businesses to the best place to work in Columbus, Ohio (according to Business First magazine). Deryck is everything DJ wanted to be, but didn't put the work in to become. Deryck learned from DJ's mistakes but left him in the past.

You have to do things like this to make it real. Make your transition into the future tangible. Change your name, your dress, your look, your attitude. Make changes that completely separate your old self from your new self. Do things that the old you would never have done. Do things that the future you will thank you for later. Do things that move you in the direction of success. Challenge yourself to be good at everything you do.

I, for one, believe that you owe it to yourself to make an effort for a fresh start. Your past does not define you nor will it continue to control you if you don't let it. You must make sure that you are in control of your own destiny. Life is a pick your own adventure book, and you get to pick the adventure that you embark on next. Will it be one that is challenging and fulfilling, or will it be much of the same? The same decisions that result in the same routines that you have been accustomed to. Sometimes you have to make yourself uncomfortable for a little while. Do different things. It feels weird at first, but these uncomfortable moments will soon become the norm. You will grow accustomed to success. The uncomfortable feeling will now be a soothing, familiar one. You will become comfortable in the skin of the new person you have become.

Why don't more people take this advice? Because it's hard! Really hard. How many times do we start things that we never finish? Books, diets, work out plans, nightly walks with our significant others? I rarely stop a diet because it's not good for me or I won't enjoy the end result; I typically stop the diet because I just simply fall off the wagon. Most people have the success gene in them, but they allow the quit gene to win. Have you ever looked back and said, "I wish I would have done that differently?" Most of the time the difference is just more effort, more focus, or both. It's hard to remain on task, especially if you are talking about a task where the only manager is yourself.

Self-management is one of the toughest characteristics to be successful at. Most of us say we can manage ourselves, but look at all of your major businesses. They all have managers, who have managers, who have managers, who report to the owner, who reports to a board or a consultant. Human nature is to procrastinate and take breaks. Human nature is holding you back, so you must do something about it. Take this book for instance. I started this book in January of 2014. The final manuscript was complete and sent to editing in June of 2018. I had a wonderful goal. 30 minutes a day. I should be able to formulate my thoughts and put them down on paper every evening for just 30 minutes. I started off fine. Every night, for roughly a week. I was one chapter in. I put the book down and didn't pick it back up until

March of that year. In March I wrote another chapter, and by April I had put the book back down. I quit my job, started a business, gained motivation, picked it back up, put it back down, and the process repeated itself for several years.

If I would have just focused and stuck to the plan, I would have accomplished this task a few years earlier. I'm not going to dwell on the past though. I'm going to learn from it and remember that when I set attainable benchmarks and realistic goals, I need to stick to the plan. After coming up with an idea, creating an implementation process for the idea, and creating a pros and cons list, I rarely believe that the idea is no good. So if the process is good, and the idea is good, you must follow through. All the way through. Finish out your plan before you make the decision that it wasn't worth it.

SETTING PROPER GOALS

"You have brains in your head. You have feet in your shoes. You can steer yourself in any direction you choose."

Dr. Seuss.

* * * * * * * *

I'm a short story guy, so I'd like to share one that has remained impactful during my career:

The Beaver and His Goals

Author: Catherine Pulsifer

It started last fall when we had a beaver move into the small stream beside our house. He immediately began taking down small trees, and within a couple of weeks our small stream turned into a small pond. Every day he added more to his damn and to his house.

The Saying Is True

We're sure you've all heard the inspirational saying, "busy as a beaver", well now we appreciate this saying as we saw the work that this beaver did over a very short period of time.

The Damn Completed

With the stream now damned and his house built, we thought that would be the last of the beaver's busy activity as winter set in. But, to our amazement, he started chewing on a very large maple tree. And, we mean large. The tree is over 60 feet tall and is approximately five feet in diameter at the base. We were amazed at the challenge this beaver was attempting. Over the winter, he would come out and chew a bit more. He had setbacks as we faced major winter storms and freezing weather. We thought that he will never chew through this tree. But sure enough, when the weather allowed, he kept coming back and would chew a bit more.

With spring finally arriving, we went down to see the beaver's progress and sure enough the tree is going to come down soon!! Our beaver has now almost completely chewed around and through the entire tree.

The Beaver's Goal

The beaver's original goal was survival - to build a home for the winter. Working every day with that particular focus in mind, he achieved that goal. But the large maple tree he started chewing on last fall was a future goal - he wanted the large tree for the spring, to provide new food and branches to continue damning in anticipation of the spring thaw. And, even with the setbacks he faced over the winter, he never gave up.

Goals Not Only For Today

Our point in sharing our beaver experience with you is to remind you that sometimes we have a goal to just survive, but we also need to set goals for tomorrow. And sometimes, just surviving seems to occupy all of our time - working everyday, looking after our family, going to school, and so forth. But, if you do just a little bit when times allows, and keep focused on your future goal, you will achieve it.

When Faced With Setbacks

It is also vitally important that when faced with setbacks in achieving a goal, you need to stay focused and not let the setbacks discourage you.

We know what it means to face setbacks along the way because we were once just like the beaver. We worked it seemed just for our survival, but we also had a future goal and we constantly kept moving forward to achieve that goal. Sometimes, though, weeks would pass before we could work on our goal again, and many times we had to deal with some sort of setback. While at times we felt we would never reach our goal, we never gave up and we never lost our focus. But, over more than 5 years, we did achieve our goal.

I can tell you from experience that it is impossible to wake up and be successful. I can tell you that it takes a ton of work, and you probably won't succeed at your first go. I can also tell you that it doesn't matter. One of the biggest factors that I attribute to my success is the ability to keep going. You have to set yourself up with proper expectations so that each benchmark feels like a win. If you are not setting proper goals, you can feel like a win is a loss and a loss is a win. Let's take a look at three major recommendations for setting goals:

First and foremost you must set goals that motivate you. Your goals have to have an end game that involves you. If you are working towards something that doesn't inspire you or doesn't cause excitement, then why are you setting this task as a goal? We need to move away from setting goals that affect your life but are done for the pleasure of other people.

We are all guilty of this. At our jobs we want to do X so that our boss is happy. In our relationships we want to do Y so that our partner is happy. As kids we want to do Z so that our parents are happy. To truly be happy, we need to do things that make us happy. Our goals should be motivational for ourselves, because let's face it, nobody can motivate us better than we can motivate ourselves.

Along with making sure the goal is important to you, you need to have a sense of urgency when it comes to accomplishing the goal. It won't be easy, so we can't procrastinate. Procrastination is the worst because it allows other things to pop into our minds. Once a goal is put off once, it's extremely easy for the goal to be put off again. Don't set yourself up for failure buy not remaining motivated to conquer your goal.

To help with this, you should have a reminder of why you want to achieve this task readily available. I like to write my "Why" on a post it note. I then place that post it note on the mirror. I brush my teeth twice a day, so twice a day, I'm reminded why I need to accomplish my goal. I highly urge you to write down your "Why" and the date you want to accomplish your goal. Keep this post it note somewhere where you will be reminded of it daily. The mirror, the bed post, your office cubicle, or anywhere that is in sight every day.

Second, we need to make an action plan on paper. This action plan should have several components to it. In the beginning of the plan, you should have specific benchmarks on the way to the end goal. These benchmarks should have deadlines. It's possible, and probable, that you will miss a deadline or two. That's OK. Put realistic time frames on each benchmark then knock them out one by one. Each accomplished benchmark will feel like a tiny battle won in an extremely long war.

Along with specific benchmarks and time frames, this action plan should have measurable check points. Having an example of "Increasing Sales," isn't very measurable. Do you want to increase sales by 1% or 100%? Do you want to have a certain amount of clients by a certain day? If so, write that down. Make sure that you are realistic with your benchmarks and goals. Having a target of 3 sales in your first month and 3000 by your second month isn't realistic. How are you going to increase sales? Will there be marketing in place? A referral program to entice word of mouth marketing? Will you have an affiliate program incorporated to try to obtain sales from different avenues?

Imagine I were to give you $86,400 dollars every day, with one stipulation, you must spend all of the money, nothing carries over to the next day. Would you spend all of the money? Most people say yes! You would wake up and spend and spend, knowing you were going to get another $86,400 tomorrow. We all have the same 86,400 seconds in a day. We just don't all spend those seconds the same. Utilize the time in an efficient manner. Get used to spending the most of those $86,400 unites every day. The ones who are at the top, have done a fantastic job at this! Do you want to be like them? If so, let's get used to squeezing every ounce out of every day.

Finally, stick to the plan! This action plan should take time to create. You should have thought and passion behind every word. You should be specific and detailed. The action plan shouldn't be done in an hour, it will probably take several days or weeks to complete. If you are going to spend time putting the perfect plan in place, you would be foolish to deviate from the plan. The plan will work, if you stick to it. It will not be easy! There will be setbacks! You will fail a few times! None of this matters though, stick to the plan, and when you feel like giving up, keep going. Trust yourself, and trust the process. If you don't accomplish your goals, what will happen? You will be forced to remain in your current situation. To change your situation, you must change your habits. Start by habitually sticking to your plan. You can thank me later.

When it comes to accomplishing goals, having unrealistic stats is a big contributor to not moving at a steady pace. If you aren't moving at a steady pace, it is easy to get sidetracked and to lose motivation. Make sure you are always working towards your goal. Celebrate the little victories, and learn from the little mistakes. Document your journey in whatever way feels the most natural, whether that be a blog, vlog, or a journal. It will be fun to go back and re-live the path that brought you to your final destination of success. You will want to have this story jotted down somewhere, so that you can share the good and bad times with yourself and others.

HALFTIME

"Think and wonder, wonder and think."

Dr. Suess.

● ● ● ● ● ● ● ●

One of my biggest secrets is to listen and then respond. Once you learn to control your reactions and outbursts, using this technique, you end up getting pretty good at listening in general. When someone, who is good at what they do, says something impactful, listen and ponder.

Before I started my own business, I had a sales manager named Al. Al had this concept to write a book called, "It's Always Halftime." The premise of the book is to talk about analyzing every segment of every decision or situation as if it were halftime. At halftime every good coach analyzes what happened in the first half, makes adjustments, and comes out with a plan to win the game. If the game we are talking about is life, then living as if it's always halftime is brilliant. Think about it:

If this **year** has been a bad **year**, then treat right now as halftime. Look back at the good and the bad. Where could you have changed things up? Where are the flaws in your plan? Now what will you do to make sure this **year** is better than last? What areas do you need to improve on? What are the steps you must take to make sure your plan works?

If this **month** has been a bad **month**, then treat right now like halftime. Look back at the good and the bad. Where could you have changed things up? Where are the flaws in your plan? Now what will you do to make sure this **month** is better than last? What areas do you need to improve on? What are the steps you must take to make sure your plan works?

If this **week** has been a bad **week**, then treat right now as halftime. Look back at the good and the bad. Where could you have changed things up? Where are the flaws in your plan? Now what will you do to make sure this **week** is better than last? What areas do you need to improve on? What are the steps you must take to make sure your plan works?

If this **day** has been a bad **day**, then treat right now as halftime. Look back at the good and the bad. Where could you have changed things up? Where are the flaws in your plan? Now what will you do to make sure this **day** is better than last? What areas do you need to improve on? What are the steps you must take to make sure your plan works?

If this **phone call...**, if this **relationship...**, if this **last 10 seconds...**, if this **business...**, if this **meal...**, etc., etc., etc.!

You must always make sure you are treating each moment as if it's halftime. Live as if it's always halftime. I loved the lesson when Al broke this down, in fact I loved it so much, I'm going to write about it. Each decision is so much more than a split reaction. Every decision that we make is important because the pattern in our decision making shapes who we are. Just as our decision of what to eat shapes our physic, the decisions on who we surround ourselves with shapes us as well. I'm a firm believer that some people are better at making decisions than others, but just like with anything, you get better the more you do something. So if you struggle to make decisions, practice. Play games that will help you improve that skill set. Go play chess! However you sharpen this skill, make sure you are acting as if it's always halftime.

Take this advice and utilize it appropriately. We don't want to be slow to act because we are going back and forth trying to decide if the decision is good or not. The point is to analyze your next decision based on the experience of your prior "half." We must be sharp and crisp. We can improve our decision making skills by actively and cognitively thinking about how to get better at making decisions in general.

I always use my business as an example. We opened our office doors in August of 2016 as an insurance agency. We had some startup funds, and we decided to invest in a cool office space that would attract employees. We knocked down walls, painted the office bright and vibrant colors, placed flat screen TVs throughout the office, ping pong table, foosball table, an area with weights and workout equipment, and more. We even bought desks that went up and down with the push of a button, so the insurance agents could sit or stand while they work.

We hired several agents, but we couldn't quite get going in terms of making steady income. We were bleeding through our startup funds, and it hadn't even been six months yet. We had to pretend it was half time and figure out what we did right and what we did wrong. We needed major adjustments, and we needed to have made those adjustments months ago. It seemed to be a little too late, and we were looking at throwing in the towel and saying, "Welp! We are out of business, but it was fun!"

I knew I had experienced sales reps, who weren't licensed to sell insurance but could sell a product if we could create one. Utilizing my deep network of those who have worked for me, or with me in the past, I was able to hire some amazing sales professionals. We sold the leads that we had purchased for our insurance agency, and marketed them as "Aged" or "Vintage" leads. We knew we could use the sponge, squeeze some water out, sell the sponge again, and the next insurance agent could potentially still squeeze some water out. It was a win-win for our agency.

The leads that we needed desperately to keep our agents writing policies would be the same leads that we would re-sell for profit. Dual purpose expenses are always great. We would buy leads for our licensed agents, and also sell those same leads to other agents to recoup our investment and turn a profit. Not that I don't love licensed agents, but there is a time hurdle of studying and obtaining the license. We didn't have that much time to wait.

Richardson Marketing Group now buys leads from vendors, specifically to re-sell to insurance agents, and we work in multiple verticals. We've serviced close to 5000 insurance agents, and we did well over a million dollars in our first two years of business. That slight adjustment, the willingness to put a plan together and hold ourselves accountable to working that plan, saved the day for me. Our insurance agency is now thriving as well. When you have multiple revenue generating businesses, it always helps. One business that literally was formed overnight, because we needed to make a halftime adjustment, really has become the more profitable of the two businesses. There is an answer, you just have to find it! You have to think of how you can solve the issue, not harp on the fact that there is an issue.

I must thank Al for this chapter. I hope to see his book one day, and if you have the chance to pick it up, it will be an extraordinary and insightful read. The mindset needed to live every day, every hour, every moment, like it's halftime, is crucial to making the decisions that your future self will thank you for. I look forward to diving deeper into the subject when his book is released.

EMBRACE THE ASSIST

"You'll miss the best things, if you keep your eyes shut."

Dr. Seuss.

● ● ● ● ● ● ● ●

The assist is a valuable part of basketball. It means you are unselfish, and you see a teammate who is in a position to make a better shot than you. It's the ultimate stat line, in my opinion. Just like I learned to live my life and make my decisions based on some techniques I've learned from others, we have to give credit where credit is due. You have to learn how to be open to other ideas and ways of doing things. On the other hand, don't be afraid to give some knowledge and information when it's appropriate. We have to use each other and learn from each other to continually grow as successful, contributing members of society.

We sometimes hoard our ideas and concepts and keep them all to ourselves. The issue is that we need to talk about these ideas, so maybe something will "click" that really starts to get that idea moving and off the ground. Maybe there is a technique or a way of doing something that you haven't tried before. Don't be afraid to mimic success, and don't be afraid to tell others to mimic you. Be a leader in life. Share what works and what doesn't work. Some people do this in networking groups, small clubs, weekly meetings with business partners and future business partners, and some even do it on the golf course with their buddies (without even knowing it).

To learn how to accept an assist, you have to be willing to listen and keep an open mind. I dabble in politics and everyone is always amazed when I say I'm a true middle of the road guy. It's extremely easy to be middle of the road when you have the willingness to listen to both sides. Just because I have Kentucky Bluegrass on my lawn, doesn't mean I don't understand why you use Perennial RyeGrass on your lawn. I may even cross the road to admire your grass. If there is an issue and somebody has a different outlook than you, close your mouth and listen to what they have to say. Actively and openly listen, and you may learn something new.

I wish I could quote the following story, but every time I look it up, it is titled with an unknown author. So I'll take the time to share one of my favorite motivational and inspirational stories of all time:

There once was a farmer who grew award winning corn. Each year he entered his corn in the state fair where it won the most prestigious award every year, The Blue Ribbon.

One year a newspaper reporter interviewed him and learned something intriguing and puzzling about how he grew this magnificent corn. The reporter discovered that the farmer shared his seed corn with his neighbors.

"How can you afford to share your best seed corn with your neighbors when they are entering the same corn competition as you each year?" the reporter asked.

"Why sir," said the farmer, "didn't you know? The wind picks up pollen from the ripening corn and swirls it from field to field. If my neighbors grow inferior corn, cross-pollination will steadily degrade the quality of my corn. If I am to grow good corn, I must help my neighbors grow good corn."

Author Unknown

This is so true in life. To be great, you need to be surrounded by greatness. If you don't have greatness around you, make it! Share your knowledge and your wealth. Show people how to do things in a more efficient manner. The greatness that you create around you will only enhance you. It's a necessary piece of this success puzzle.

Another one of my favorite quotes is:

"It is possible to give away and become richer! It is also possible to hold on too tightly and lose everything. Yes, the liberal man shall be rich! By watering down others, he waters himself."

Proverbs 11:24-24

The Holy Bible

When our parents told us to, "Go Play," we were able to share toys with our siblings or share ideas and games with the other kids in the neighborhood. We just don't do this often enough as an adult. Soak up information and ideas. If we are to grow good corn, we must help our neighbors grow good corn. If we are to live well, we must help other live well. We are an average of the five closest people to us, help to raise the level of the ocean and make the other four as good as possible. Then reach your arm out and touch more people. You will reap the value of being a teacher and influencer. It's just how this world works.

I love sharing knowledge and learning from others. While running sales teams I've always talked about what can be done to make my guys better. Instead of acting like a sales rep, act like a CEO. Make decisions that will benefit the company and make the company grow. As the company grows so will you. The healthier the company, the more comfortable you will be working here.

One of my favorite small study groups was Future CEO's of America. We started this at an inside sales organization I was running several years ago, and I've taken it with me to another employer and now to both of my businesses. It's a lunch where we take time away from our day to learn and get to know traits of others who aspire to be in leadership. There have been different formats over the years, but essentially we order pizza and discuss topics that are going on within the company and go around the room to see how we would handle the issues.

Leadership slowly started coming to these meetings, as they knew every Wednesday we were positively discussing creative ideas to make the company healthier. In the beginning it was just the sales manager, then soon the directors, VP's, and Presidents would listen in on these meetings. We are able to positively move things forward by empowering those people who wanted experience in these types of situations.

We did not prohibit anyone from coming to the meetings, but we slowly found out who would come regularly and engage and impact the meetings and who wasn't at all interested. Attendance has no bearings on promotions, and it's clear to everyone that you do not have to attend these meetings. The valuable information that was learned was who thought the collaboration was a silly idea. FCA was shunned by some who had management experience, but found themselves in a non-management role. The attitude that, "I don't need this, I know how to lead," said a lot when looking to promote these same people in the future. Though attendance is never necessary, your attitude towards a program that helps to enhance skills does. One person in particular was extremely irate that he was passed up for a management opening for a younger person with no leadership experience. He blamed FCA and said the reason he was passed up was because, and I quote, "he didn't waste his Wednesdays with a group of people who are brown nosing and sucking up to boost their career."

The young millennial who was put in that management position over the veteran manager now owns a multimillion dollar business and is an incredible CEO. We have collaborated on some co-op deals, and he is nothing but a pleasure to work with. It often reminds me of the Wednesday FCA meetings that he attended regularly. I'll never forget the one week I was on vacation, and I asked him to facilitate the meeting. His eyes were as big as baseballs with excitement. He told me he would not let me down, and he would make sure the hour was spent in a productive manner. Not once did he ask me what I wanted him to do. He took the project and ran. He went to "Go Play."

When I returned the group was eager to let me know how great of a time they had with this employee running the meeting. This prompted us to rotate facilitators of the meetings, so someone different was in charge each week. The best feeling in the world is watching the nerves disappear from a young up and coming leader right before your eyes. Once they get into a groove some people are naturals. Some people aren't, and to see them work extremely hard at getting better is just as rewarding.

Receiving an assist should always be reciprocated. You either give back to the person who assisted you, or you pay it forward and provide an assist to someone else. Each situation is different and I assure you that you will learn to do a bit of both. Become the person you want to be, learn the things that will get you there, find someone with similar aspirations, and show them how you have gotten so far. Make sure you wake up every morning with purpose, and learn something new, or share something new every single day!

THE END GAME

"*Think left and think right and think low and think high. Oh, the things you can think up if only you try.*"

Dr. Seuss.

* * * * * * * *

Putting everything together sounds easier than it truly is. The biggest thing that you have to do is motivate yourself to do it! The subtitle of this book is, "The Ultimate Road Map to Winning the Game of Life." Everyone's life is different, making everyone's end-game different. Some people strive to own businesses, others strive to climb the corporate later, some strive to finish their degree, or get married, or have children, or buy a new house, or buy a new car, or move to a new city, the list of what motivates each individual goes on and on. I've said it a million times, dangling a carrot in front of a horse does nothing if the horse doesn't like carrots.

With this being the case, the only person who truly knows who motivates you, is you. The only person who really knows what you want, is you. The only person who truly knows what is going to make you move and get the ball rolling, is you! Maybe you haven't figured out any of this yet; the good news is, you can figure it out buy talking to yourself and asking, "Self, what do we want to do in life?" Once we figure this part out, we want to learn what it takes to get to where we want to go. Research, just like your school days, will be vital in figuring out if the future you want is truly something attainable.

Are your expectations realistic? To find this out, you may want to reach out to someone who has done what you are trying to do. People enjoy talking about themselves and their journey. Invite someone to lunch, or reach out via email. Pick their brain. Remember our "Assist" chapter? Most people who have found success, the type someone would strive to achieve, don't mind giving an assist. Don't be too shy to ask what exactly it's like to be the person you strive to be. One of the worst things you could do is to work extremely hard at a goal, just to get to said goal, and the feeling isn't exactly what you thought it would be. This happens more times than you may think.

Once we have realistic expectations, now we need to create a plan to get us to the end of the road. Write in to the plan the speed bumps that are going to happen. It's inevitable, speed bumps will come, it doesn't matter how well written your plan, or how well thought out your plan. Prepare for the rough ride, buckle up, anything worth having is not easy! Go into your journey knowing this and write your plan accordingly. Again, often time the journey is more fulfilling than the outcome, enjoy the ride! Learn from the mistakes. Take good notes so that, if need be, you can go through this again, or teach someone how to get where you are. One day the roles will be reversed and you will be handing out the assist to someone desperately needing the information so that they may start their own, similar journey.

Once you make it, don't forget where you came from. Give back. Become an influencer in your community. Volunteer. Do not take your success in stride. Karma is real, and she doesn't play fair when you don't play fair. Do it the right way. Spend time analyzing everything and putting plans together. Write down your goals, check off benchmarks as you complete them, and never give up. It sounds extremely easy, and it is for the first few days, but it gets harder to stay consistent. Keep that in mind. Think of the gyms that are completely full on January 1st, but empty, or at least back to normal attendance, by February 15th. It is literally a mental challenge to make a goal and stay excited about achieving that goal as it becomes less enjoyable and more of a struggle. Staying on pace, in itself, is a benchmark that should be checked off.

The feeling of reaching top of your proverbial mountain will be worth it. If you have ever set a goal, and accomplished that goal, it is a rush that is better than the feeling of any drug. You will become a celebrity within your own circle of people as most of them have probably failed at some sort of goal. Don't sweat it though, encourage them, and become an influencer to their journey. We all fail. Success is measured by "1". Get up one more time than you got knocked down. Try again one more time than you failed. Believe it or not, you will get used to failing and bouncing back. The bounce back portion of this journey is critical to keeping you motivated. Get very good at failing and bouncing back; you will need that endurance. Get prepared for the uncomfortable feeling of not succeeding right away. Find comfort in that uncomfortable feeling. I've always said, "When I'm comfortable, my family is uncomfortable. When I'm uncomfortable, my family is comfortable." As the head of my household I've embraced that mentality for many years, and it is the primary driving force of my hustle.

The final topic I'm going to discuss is going to be the most important. Don't listen to people who want you to fail! There will be plenty of people who are your friends or family who support you, and there will be people who are your friends or family who don't. Watch their actions and their words. Your true team will believe in you, no matter what. There is a saying that, "No man is a profit in his own land." This essentially means, you can't be a superstar around your own circle of friends. Some of these people close to you will be ready to embrace your newfound change, others won't. It's not a big deal. Don't allow the naysayers to hold you back. Let them know early that you know this is hard, and you are willing to face the failures and challenges that will come up during this journey. It's OK for them to be by your side, and it's ok for them not to believe in you. It's not OK to sabotage what you are doing. You control the energy you accept in your life; do not allow negative energy in at this point in your life. It won't work.

Another one of my favorite stories is that of the Deaf Frog:

Once upon a time, there was a group of tiny frogs who arranged a competition. The goal was to reach the top of a tower. A huge crowd of frogs gathered to watch the race and cheer on the contestants.

The race began.

Not one frog in the audience believed that the contestants would reach to the top. After all, it was a HUGE tower! The crowd grew and many yelled,

"Oh, that is WAY too difficult!!"

"They will NEVER make it to the top."

"Not a chance that they will succeed. The tower is too high!"

One by one, the tiny frogs collapsed and fell off the tower. Still, there was a group of determined frogs that climbed higher and higher. But the crowd continued to yell,

"It is too difficult!!! No one will make it!"

Discouraged and convinced by the negative cries, more of these tiny frogs collapsed and fell off the tower. Many frogs who were still climbing complained of the pain and eventually gave up. Some frogs, tired and battered, heard their peers' complaints and subsequently threw in the towel too.

In the midst of this, ONE tiny frog persisted. He climbed. And he climbed. And he climbed. This tiny frog seemed to have super-frog strength that allowed him to push forward in spite of others failing. Why, though? Why is he able to climb so far when others are failing?? the crowd wondered.

By now, all the tiny frogs had either collapsed or given up — except for that one tiny frog. The crowd continued to yell, now at the tiny frog:

"This is too difficult!!'

"You will NEVER make it to the top!!"

"You better give up now while you can!!!"

But for some reason, that tiny frog climbed further, seemingly undaunted, unaffected. Finally, he reached the top of the hill. He had reached his destination!!!

All the tiny frogs were amazed that this one frog was able to make it to the top. They crowded around him, wanting to know his secret.

As it turned out, he was deaf.

And so as we end the motivational section of this book, I encourage you to be good at being deaf! Don't listen to the negatives that will come up while you are ascending your climb. The possible is possible. In fact, aerodynamically, the bumblebee should not be able to fly. Google it! The problem is, the bumblebee doesn't know this, so he flies daily. Go Fly! Good luck on your flight. I'll be cheering for you for sure! Also, go play. You'll fall and have some grass stains to scrub out. It will be tough, but so rewarding all in the same breath. Go play. Bring others with you on your journey. Go play. Go be an inspiration. Prove that you can accomplish your goals and then show others they can do it to. Go play. Be impactful. Go play. Be an influencer. Go play and have fun!

ABOUT THE AUTHOR

"Today you are you, that is truer than true. There is no one alive that is youer than you!"

Dr. Seuss

● ● ● ● ● ● ● ●

My father is an immigrant from Nassau, Bahamas. Dr. Deryck Richardson Sr. came to Columbus, Ohio to get his PhD from The Ohio State University. He never left the Columbus area after meeting my mother. Though my mom, Nadya, has a lot of cultures that account for her extremely fair skin, she was born in the 40s, and back then any hint of African American heritage forced you to identify as black. My mom was very much a firecracker and very stern and strong in her matriarch duties. My father was a hustler. He started his own private practice as a clinical psychologist and also held other positions along the way. He always had a "side hustle," whether it was teaching courses at Ohio State or adjudicating claims for the Bureau of Disability Determination.

When I was younger, I didn't realize the amount of hustle my father had, in fact we really didn't identify with each other for many years. I was very much trying to fit in to our mostly white suburban neighborhood. Doing so in the 90's was tough as I was often times too dark for the white kids and too light for the black kids. I definitely didn't sound like the black kids as my household has always been well spoken. This identity crisis will be touched on a little later.

My mother had 2 daughters from previous marriages, but I never heard the word "step" in our house. In fact, both of my sisters called my father Dad, and I couldn't even tell you how old I was when I realized we were technically half siblings. I was my parents' first biological child, and three years later my brother would complete the fabulous four. My sisters are 18 years and 10 years older than I am, so for most of my childhood it was just me and my younger brother. My brother and I, though growing up tight, were completely different as kids. I was into sports, girls, rap music, not doing homework, etc. My brother was an actor, writer, musician, and just downright ultra-talented in anything he did. I often wondered why he didn't want to just play sports, he would have dominated if he put his mind to it, but he didn't want to. I thought that was a little weird at times; boy do I wish maybe I would have followed his path instead.

I'm not sure if my parents knew how much I struggled in my younger years. I was one of just a handful of black kids, I have always been overweight, and I'm just not a fighter, so I would avoid conflict when kids would tease me, rather than confront it. I remember one time I was in a fight and came home with scratches on my face. My mom asked what I did back to the kid, and I said nothing. She proceeded to scream and yell at me and tell me that I had to fight back, or I would be in more trouble when I returned home. I took her advice, but learned to fight with my words rather than my fists. I've probably been in three physical altercations in my entire life, it's just not my thing.

My self-esteem really blossomed and took off when I began to play football. My body was just made for the sport, and when you are good at sports, people tend to want to be around you. With these new people wanting to be my friends I began to find myself and really find my identity. I could now be myself without fears of bullying or retribution. It was a great feeling that has stuck with me throughout adulthood. High school came, and I was focused on hanging out with people and doing whatever was popular at the time, even if it wasn't the best decisions. I wasn't a hoodlum or anything, never in trouble with the law, but I definitely had plenty of drunken escapades and smoked a lot of marijuana in my teens. I thought what it meant to be black was to sag my pants, listen to blaring music, smoke weed, and hang out all night. It wasn't who I was, my brother was cut from the same cloth and didn't act like that. It was just who I thought I had to be. Possibly the media influenced me as this was the rise of MTV and BET showing videos of young black males acting this way. Who knows.

I always worked. At 14 years old I was riding my bike in a strip mall and there was a Help Wanted sign in what looked like an office. It was a call center where the owners would hire teenagers to do telemarketing. 90's telemarketing, "Boiler Room" style telemarketing, asking people for straight donations to the Police Athletic League and Fraternal Order of Police. We were one of those outfits that gave about 3% of what we raised to the organizations we were representing and kept the other 97% for "operating expenses." I would work in this industry on and off through high school, taking a break during my sports seasons and coming back and jumping right back in to the groove of being a top producer. There was a rush in making commissions. My friends were working at McDonalds and the local grocery store for minimum wage (five dollars an hour at the time), and I was clearing several hundred per week, sometimes as much as $600.

When high school ended I decided if I wasn't going to play football, there was no reason to continue my education in college. Afterall, I was less into books and more into hanging out. I was making good money, I could get an apartment and hang out whenever I wanted without the rules of my parents. I could be living the life at 18! That "life" would put me in a very unique situation that really shaped the man I am today. I would wind up being a statistic. A teenage father. I was now 19 with a baby to raise. Uh-Oh, time to grow up!

The relationship with my daughter's mother was toxic. I think she meant well, but she just wasn't ready to grow up like I was. I was writing down goals and coming up with plans to make more money for my family. She continued to party. I remember coming home from work, and my daughter was in her room by herself. Her mother's argument was she needed a nap; I just couldn't stand to see my daughter lonely like that. I needed to save her from the situation we were in. $400 dollars a week was nothing now that I had an apartment and mouths to feed. I needed to do something, and my daughter would come with me, but her mother was no longer welcome on my journey.

I went through a brief custody battle. I believe my daughter's mother put up more of a fight because her family expected her to. Again, I don't think she doesn't love our daughter, now or back then, I just think she was ready to keep being young, and I had started my success journey. I fought against her family trying to take custody of my daughter, and I have had custody ever since she was three years old. My family was fabulous in helping me raise her. I was a 22 year old male with dreams and aspirations. I had no idea how to raise a kid. I just knew how to love her and make decisions that would benefit her and I as we clawed through life.

I put myself through college after I was awarded custody of my daughter. Still working on the phones, I was an appointment setter for a mortgage company and going to school during the day. I leaned heavily on my older sisters, who now had kids of their own, and my mother to help watch my daughter as I prepared myself for my life journey. I couldn't have done anything without them, I don't know if they know how grateful I truly am.

I graduated from Ohio Dominican University and started looking for a "real job." I told my boss, at the mortgage company, that I would be leaving once I found a higher paying gig. He told me, "You aren't going anywhere. You are a natural on the phone and a natural born leader. I'm going to pay for your mortgage license and show you how to manage a team." I was honored and gladly accepted this assist. Again, when someone offers an assist, take it!

I was 26 and making six figures in the mortgage business. I was finally on my feet financially and my daughter was thriving in school. I met my wife at this time in my life, and it was another blessing that is appreciated tremendously. She had kids and already knew how to be a mother. I tell people all the time that I may wear the pants in my house but my wife picks out my clothes every day! We quickly combined our families and I went from a single father of one, to a married man with four kids in the matter of a few years.

Unfortunately, just as my new family was getting settled together, the mortgage market, specifically the sub-prime market in which I was managing a division of the mortgage company, fell out. We were all out of jobs overnight. I had a brilliant idea. I've always wanted to teach, so I decided I'd go be a teacher and start a business on the side. The hours of teaching would allow me to be in by 3:30 pm every day, off weekends, and off during the summer. We decided that my wife would be a homemaker, and we would struggle for a second while I focused on getting my business off the ground. I'll never forget my mother in law coming over one day to look at our finances because we were struggling so bad. She left without any advice because she said it was a miracle we weren't homeless.

Remember I went from six figures to a teacher's salary overnight. Our savings quickly dwindled. We lost our five bedroom house with our three car garage. We lost our cars. We had nights that the electricity was disconnected. The kids thought dad "forgot to pay the bill." We struggled. It was a purposeful struggle; we knew this would happen. I needed my wife to be at home with the kids while I built my business. I needed to use bill money to invest in products. Guess what happened to my first business. It failed! Right after I stopped teaching. I knew we had everything right, yet the business failed within a year.

By now, we had learned to live on the lower income and the impact of this business failing didn't hit the "house" as hard as before. We learned our lesson and tried not to repeat mistakes. We bought modest vehicles instead of luxury ones, the house we rented in 2010, we still live in as of publication of this book in 2019. I'm well on my feet now, but that is the "home" my children know. There was no reason to move away from their neighborhood just because we had some success. The excess funds would begin to go to our rainy day fund and allow us to take more chances and fail more.

I eventually found a job in lead generation as a sales manager. I've always been in sales and sales management, so it felt good to have some nice money coming in again, but it didn't feel nice knowing I was building someone else's business. I literally would preach in my sales meetings about acting like a CEO and not giving up on your dreams. All the motivational stuff I would tell my staff in the meetings really hit home because I wasn't living that life. I decided to make a change and jump again.

I went to work one day, not knowing it would be my last day; I had just had enough. Enough of not being able to truly shine in the way I knew I could.

Enough of helping my boss become a millionaire. Enough of having to worry about missing my kids' games, while telling my employees they needed to set their priorities so they weren't missing work. I just had enough. My business partner had tried to recruit me to build an insurance agency with him for about two years anyway. I was ready to do this business thing again.

Guess what though? We failed! Again. We failed. This time, we had a backup plan in place though. After getting our office set up and hiring employees and getting procedures in place, we failed. Terribly. We could have been out of business in less than a year if we weren't able to pivot and build a second company under the same roof. This one would have hurt more than before because so many people were actually pulling for us to succeed. Failure, this time, was not an option. So we pivoted, found a solution and a way to make money, and our second business was born.

Today, both businesses are thriving, and I couldn't be more happy. My kids are positive contributing members of society, and my free time has opened up to allow me to give back. I'm president of our local youth club and run the basketball program there. I am super involved in the community and running campaigns for local people who are truly trying to make a difference. I am a mentor to those who want to get to the next level of their lives and their journeys.

I'm playing, now it's your turn. Go Play!

CPSIA information can be obtained
at www.ICGtesting.com
Printed in the USA
LVHW040957020320
648681LV00004B/583